HI-D

A Stage Play

by Paul Carpenter and Ian Gower

‖SAMUEL FRENCH‖

samuelfrench.co.uk

FOR AMATEUR PRODUCTION ENQUIRIES

UNITED KINGDOM AND WORLD
EXCLUDING NORTH AMERICA
plays@samuelfrench.co.uk
020 7255 4302/01

Each title is subject to availability from Samuel French,
depending upon country of performance.

THINKING ABOUT PERFORMING A SHOW?

There are thousands of plays and musicals available to perform from Samuel French right now, and applying for a licence is easier and more affordable than you might think

From classic plays to brand new musicals, from monologues to epic dramas, there are shows for everyone.

Plays and musicals are protected by copyright law, so if you want to perform them, the first thing you'll need is a licence. This simple process helps support the playwright by ensuring they get paid for their work and means that you'll have the documents you need to stage the show in public.

Not all our shows are available to perform all the time, so it's important to check and apply for a licence before you start rehearsals or commit to doing the show.

LEARN MORE & FIND THOUSANDS OF SHOWS

Browse our full range of plays and musicals, and find out more about how to license a show
www.samuelfrench.co.uk/perform

Talk to the friendly experts in our Licensing team for advice on choosing a show and help with licensing
plays@samuelfrench.co.uk   020 7387 9373

Acting Editions

BORN TO PERFORM

Playscripts designed from the ground up to work the way you do in rehearsal, performance and study

---

Larger, clearer text for easier reading

Wider margins for notes

Performance features such as character and props lists, sound and lighting cues, and more

---

+ CHOOSE A SIZE AND STYLE TO SUIT YOU

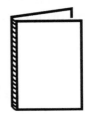

STANDARD EDITION

SPIRAL-BOUND EDITION

LARGE EDITION

Our regular paperback book at our regular size

The same size as the Standard Edition, but with a sturdy, easy-to-fold, easy-to-hold spiral-bound spine

A4 size and spiral bound, with larger text and a blank page for notes opposite every page of text – perfect for technical and directing use

---

| LEARN MORE | samuelfrench.co.uk/actingeditions

HI-DE-HI!

First presented by Tring Festival Company at The Court Theatre, Tring, Hertfordshire, on 19th June 2007 with the following cast and creative team:

GLADYS PUGH	Stephanie Bedwin
BETTY WHISTLER	Pippa Nash
GARY	Matt Bowles
DAWN	Deborah Berry
TRACY BENTWOOD	Kelly Winter
PEGGY OLLERENSHAW	Maxine Reece
JEFFREY FAIRBROTHER	Andy Faber
FRED QUILLY	Ray Brown
YVONNE STUART-HARGREAVES	Eileen Reece
BARRY STUART-HARGREAVES	Paul Stratford
TED BOVIS	Dennis Fugard
SPIKE DIXON	Colin Hubbocks
MR PARTRIDGE	Steve Berry
SYLVIA GARNSEY	Regina Dobbs
HILARY BOVIS	Ginny Faber
BAILIFF	Ian Muirhead
MR PRITCHARD	Dave Barratt

Executive Producer Ian Gower
Directed by Paul Carpenter
Designed by Bruce Sherring-Lucas
Lighting designed by Mike Sherring-Lucas
Costumes by Emma Bunting

CHARACTERS

GLADYS PUGH

BETTY WHISTLER

GARY DAWN

TRACY BENTWOOD

PEGGY OLLERENSHAW

JEFFREY FAIRBROTHER

FRED QUILLY

MR PARTRIDGE

YVONNE STUART-HARGREAVES

BARRY STUART-HARGREAVES

TED BOVIS

SPIKE DIXON

SYLVIA GARNSEY

HILARY BOVIS

BAILIFF

MR PRITCHARD

SYNOPSIS OF SCENES

The action of the play takes place at Maplins Holiday Camp, Crimpton-on-Sea.

Prologue "Radio Maplin" Desk

ACT I

Scene One   Staff Room and Office, morning.
Scene Two   "Radio Maplin" Desk, that afternoon.
Scene Three Staff Room and Office, later that afternoon.
Scene Four   Side Area of the Ballroom, that evening.
Scene Five   Staff Chalets, later that evening.

ACT II

Scene One   Staff Chalets, the following morning.
Scene Two   Ballroom Stage, later that morning.
Scene Three "Radio Maplin" Desk, later that morning.
Scene Four   Staff Room and Office, that lunchtime.
Scene Five   Ballroom Stage, three days later.
Scene Six   Bar, later that afternoon.
Scene Seven Ballroom Stage, later that afternoon.
Scene Eight   Staff Room and Office, later that afternoon.

Time—1950s.

PROLOGUE

Radio Maplin Desk Area at Maplins Holiday Camp. 1950s.

The lights come up in front of the tabs on a radio desk with a chair, a xylophone and xylophone stick. There is a record player with a record on it. Late 50s music is playing and sounds like it's coming from a muffled tannoy.

GLADYS enters left and sits at the desk. She lifts off the record. The music stops.

Yellowcoats BETTY, GARY, DAWN and TRACY come on from each side of the audience and stand in front of the tabs. As GLADYS speaks they indicate where the exits are and react to photography and mobile phone warnings.

GLADYS plays the notes C G E on the xylophone.

GLADYS Hello campers—hi-de-hi! *(She waits for the audience "ho-de-ho" response)* Oh, you can do better than that, HI-DE-HI!

"Ho-de-ho!"

That's much better. This is Gladys Pugh, your Radio Maplin's announcer. We've a packed programme ahead of you today at Maplins. But first of all some safety announcements. The fire exits are located either side of the stage and where you came in to the Hawaiian Ballroom. And while you are here, no flash photography, it's very distracting to the yellowcoats. We hope you have a lovely time here at Maplins Holiday

Camp. *(Deadpan)* Oh. I nearly forgot, please make sure you turn off those mobile phones. Hi-de-hi!

"Ho-de-ho!"

(she plays the notes C G E on the xylophone again) Thank you, Yellowcoats, now to your places.

GLADYS *exits via the tabs. The Yellowcoats exit via the audience.*

The lights go down on the desk area.

Open tabs.

ACT I

Scene One

The Staff Room and Office. Morning.

The lights come up on a composite set comprising the staff room and office. There are entrances to the staff room through a back door and a side door. There is another door between the two rooms. In the staff room is a table with tea and coffee utensils, cups, sugar cubes and a tray on it, chairs, an armchair and a transistor radio. In the office is a desk with two telephones on it, two chairs, a filing cabinet, duty board and a window.

JEFFREY is standing in the office by the window reading a letter. He is wearing an overcoat over his shirt but has no trousers on.

PEGGY enters the staff room by the back door carrying a pair of trousers. She knocks on the office door.

PEGGY Mr Fairbrother, are you decent?

JEFFREY Just a minute. *(He adjusts his overcoat and opens the door)* Come in, Peggy.

PEGGY I've brought your trousers. I've pressed them and they've got a knife-edged crease.

JEFFREY Good.

PEGGY Fancy that kid getting porridge all down them. Oh, and there was a ten bob note in one of the pockets. It was a bit old, so I pressed that as well. *(She hands JEFFREY a note. It is stiff as a board)* Er, hi-de-hi!

JEFFREY Yes, and er, ho-de-ho!

> **PEGGY** *leaves by the side door, as* **GLADYS** *arrives by the back door.*

PEGGY *(passing* **GLADYS***)* Hi-de-hi!

> **PEGGY** *exits.*

JEFFREY Ah, good morning, Gladys.

> **GLADYS** *closes the door behind her.* **JEFFREY** *lifts the trousers up against his body discreetly.*

GLADYS You haven't forgotten the staff meeting is five minutes earlier today.

JEFFREY No, no, I haven't forgotten.

> **GLADYS** *looks down at* **JEFFREY***'s trousers.*

GLADYS Did you sleep well?

JEFFREY Yes, yes, the air here is marvellous.

GLADYS *(still looking down)* From what I saw of you last night, it wasn't only the air that made you sleep.

> **JEFFREY** *looks down and rather nervously pulls up the trouser zip and holds them closer to his body.*

JEFFREY Some of the campers will insist on buying me drinks. I've been trying to avoid some lads down from my old university.

GLADYS I hear Sylvia bought you one too, didn't she?

JEFFREY Yes, well, she had a win on the fruit machine.

GLADYS Fruit machine's been out of order three weeks. You want to be careful. Joe Maplin doesn't like management drinking with Yellowcoats. Especially her. *(She turns to go)* You coming then?

JEFFREY No, no, I can't, Gladys. I haven't got any trousers on.

GLADYS *(turning)* Oh, I'm sorry. I hadn't noticed.

> GLADYS *closes the door behind her and leaves office and staff room by the side door as* FRED QUILLY *enters by the back door wearing full jockey gear and carrying a shoulder bag.*

> JEFFREY *puts on his trousers and sits at the desk looking at paperwork.*

> *The lights go down on the office.*

> FRED *goes over to the table upstage left where the tea and coffee cups are located. He looks about him and starts to collect sugar cubes and put them into his pockets.*

> PEGGY *enters by the side door.*

PEGGY Hello, Fred.

> FRED *is startled.*

What are you up to?

FRED N-nothing.

PEGGY Come on, what have you been putting in your pockets?

FRED N-n-nothing.

PEGGY Come on, show me.

FRED Just a few lumps of sugar.

PEGGY *(looking in his pockets)* What are you talking about, there's nearly half a pound in there.

FRED It's for my horses, they don't get much out of life. They get up in the morning—well, they're already up. That's because they sleep standing up. Then they're out trekking everyday with them great heavy campers on their backs, and all they see is the back of the horse in front of them. How'd you like to spend your life plodding along, looking at the arse of an 'orse.

PEGGY Oh, poor things. Oh, take the rest, I can get some more.

Smiling, **FRED** *scoops up all the remaining lumps and puts them in his bag.*

PEGGY *arranges cups and departs by the side door as* **YVONNE** *and* **BARRY** *waft in by the back door wearing their dancing gear. They head towards the tea and coffee table.*

FRED *moves back slightly.*

YVONNE No, Barry, I just couldn't face eating that ghastly bacon, it was swimming in fat. If I ate it I would have one of my stomachs again.

BARRY I do hope you're going to be fit tonight. Last night you were as stiff as a board.

YVONNE Well, as you know I have a very delicate back...

BARRY ...It was like dancing with a docker.

YVONNE You would have more experience of that than I.

They approach the coffee table. **YVONNE** *picks up a cup.*

Just look at these cups, they're filthy.

BARRY Well, as my mother always said, we all eat a peck of dirt before we die, dear.

YVONNE The way she ran the house, you must have fulfilled your quota years ago.

They turn away from each other at the coffee table.

TED *enters by the back door.*

TED *(calling off)* Spike! Spike! I told you that costume was a bad idea. What did I tell you? First rule of comedy, realism.

SPIKE *enters by the back door wearing a dustbin costume, complete with lid hat. The bin has porridge drips down the side of it.*

(Examining the costume) This costume...it's rubbish!

SPIKE What are you talking about? I was doing all right over breakfast, I had them all singing *My Old Man's A Dustman* until one kid started emptying his breakfast into me—then they all joined in the fun. I had to crouch down and put me lid on.

TED *approaches* **BARRY** *and* **YVONNE.**

TED How's Fred Astaire and Ginger Rogers this morning?

Yellowcoats **SYLVIA** , **DAWN, TRACY** *and* **GARY** *enter and wait at the rear of the staff room. Each take a cup and talk amongst themselves.*

YVONNE Ignore him, Barry. *(She hands* **BARRY** *a cup)*

TED What are you doing ponced up at this time of day for?

YVONNE We happen to be doing some private tuition this morning.

TED *takes the cup out of* **BARRY**'s *hand and goes to sit in the armchair.*

MR PARTRIDGE *enters by the back door, obviously in a bad mood, muttering. He approaches* **TED** *sitting in the armchair.*

MR PARTRIDGE *(to* **TED***)* Oi! Do you mind! I always sit here!

TED *gets up out of armchair to allow* **MR PARTRIDGE** *to sit.*

TED You're in a crabby mood this morning.

MR PARTRIDGE Yeah, and so would you be if you had to share a chalet with him. *(Pointing to* **FRED***)* It's like living in a blasted stable.

FRED *(collecting two cups)* There's nothing the matter with the smell of horses, mate. I have to put up with your nightmares. *(He hands* **MR PARTRIDGE** *a cup)*

MR PARTRIDGE Oh, I had a terrible one last night. I was doing me Punch and Judy show and the crocodile kept getting bigger and bigger and bigger. And then it ate me. It was horrible. I shall have to stop working with that crocodile you know.

GLADYS *enters from the side door carrying a yellow envelope.*

GLADYS Now, everybody, Mr Fairbrother will be along directly.

SYLVIA *(mimicking)* Mr Fairbrother will be along directly.

GLADYS *stops to glare at* **SYLVIA.** *She knocks on the office door.*

The lights come up on the office.

BARRY I think she's got one of those letters from our founder, Joe Maplin.

TED How do you know?

BARRY I detected one of his tasteful envelopes. Yellow, with a pink candy stripe border.

JEFFREY *rises, heads towards the door and opens it.*

JEFFREY Good morning, everybody.

ALL Good morning.

JEFFREY Thank you. I shan't be a tick, and erm, hi-de-hi!

ALL Ho-de-ho!

GLADYS *and* **JEFFREY** *step back into the office.*

PEGGY *returns by the side door and quietly replenishes the sugar bowl with lumps.*

GLADYS *(handing over the letter)* Here's another letter from Joe Maplin for you to read to the staff.

JEFFREY Oh good lord, I find it so embarrassing. Can I use my own words this time? *(He opens the letter and scans it quickly)*

GLADYS No. It might get back to him. He likes them read out exactly as he dictates them to his secretary.

JEFFREY Very well.

JEFFREY *leads* **GLADYS** *to the door.*

GLADYS I see you've got your trousers on.

JEFFREY *stops at the door and turns, a puzzled look on his face.*

They hang beautifully.

JEFFREY *slowly leaves the office.*

The lights go down on the office.

The staff all gather facing **JEFFREY.** **GLADYS** *joins him at his side.* **PEGGY** *busies herself with some dusting behind the group.*

JEFFREY I'm going to start the meeting. I received a letter from Joe Maplin this morning. I don't know about you, but I really do enjoy reading these letters, 'cos, erm, 'cos Joe writes as he thinks, and they really are, er, sincere. *(Reading)* "Get this into your thick heads." That, that's the letter, it's not me... *(Reading)* "You got to pull your socks up about your pool fun. Last week I dropped in on the Warmsley Camp, that was Sunday afternoon and their pool fun were pathetic. No one was ducking anyone, and no one was chucking anyone in. Get this. I want plenty of ducking and chucking, and not so much loafing around. Let's have some new gimmicks. Neptunes and octopusses is old hat." He means octopi, he's got pussies, it's not right. *(Reading)* "How's this for starters. Host throws comic in. Comic grabs host by ankle and pulls him in. Punch and Judy man dives in to save them.

MR PARTRIDGE *reacts.*

"Riding instructor dives in to save Punch and Judy man.

FRED *reacts.*

"Dancing instructors do tango, slip on a banana skin, go in.

YVONNE *and* **BARRY** *react.*

"Continue dancing in the water. I want to see the whole surface of the pool covered in bobbing heads, shouting help and pretending to drown." Yes, well, I think we all get the gist of what Mr Maplin has in mind...

MR PARTRIDGE Well I'm not going in the pool at my time of life.

FRED He'll shrivel up.

YVONNE Who is going to pay for the costumes?

BARRY What about my sinuses? The chloride'll play havoc with them.

YVONNE The whole idea's absurd.

PEGGY *(rushing forward)* I don't mind going in the pool.

GLADYS You're not supposed to be here, Peggy. Get on with your work.

PEGGY I've got to wash these cups up.

> **PEGGY** *picks up the tray and tidies up, then departs by the side door.*

SPIKE Look, I'm the one that gets thrown in the pool, Mr Fairbrother. If everyone goes in I shall look an idiot.

All turn to look at **SPIKE** *in his dustbin costume.*

JEFFREY Well don't worry, anyone. What we have to do is adapt this to our own particular needs. If any of you do have any ideas about, er, pool wheezes, don't hesitate and bring them straight to me.

TED That's a good idea. "Jeffrey Fairbrother—wheeze in the pool".

JEFFREY *smiles. Then the penny drops!*

JEFFREY Er, there's more. It's, er, not all bad news. *(Reading)* "Before I ends, you done a swell job last season. But this year you got to top it. And then some." ...And then some. It's still in his own words of course, it's not, erm, it's not me. Er... *(Reading)* "Yellowcoats." Yellowcoats—that's you. *(Reading)* "You got to keep them smiles flashing. Last time I were around the camps there were too many funeral faces."

MR PARTRIDGE It can't be me he's talking about. Nobody sees me. I'm always down here all the time with me Punch and Judy in the air. *(He demonstrates by putting his hands in the air)*

YVONNE I take it he's not referring to us.

BARRY You can't demonstrate the slow foxtrot, grinning like Bugs Bunny.

YVONNE You have to have a dignified expression on your face.

FRED Yer, like you got a nasty smell under your nose.

BARRY Mmmm, in your case, you usually have.

BETTY He can't mean us either, can he, girls?

All the girls agree.

DAWN No, we spend all day smiling at the campers.

JEFFREY Yes, yes, yes, I am sure there are exceptions. But what Mr Maplin says is right in principle. And that's why he's where he is today.

TED Aye. That and paying us in washers.

JEFFREY All right, all right. I'll just read on. *(Reading)* "And don't forget to ram home my catchphrase, hi-de-hi. After all, I was the one what invented it."

MR PARTRIDGE He never invented it. It was that mad colonel during the war. He shouted out hi-de-hi and the soldiers had to shout ho-de-ho back. He got court-martialled for it.

JEFFREY Yes, yes, but that's neither here nor there, Mr Partridge. *(Reading)* "From now on, every Thursday will be Sunshine Smile day, and any member of the staff found not smiling anytime from Wakey Wakey to Goodnight Campers will be out on their..." yes, well, Mr Maplin certainly doesn't mince his words. *(Reading)* "And I don't want a smirk or a grin, but a full smile with flashing molars. Go to it, hi-de-hi! Joe Maplin." Well, of course you see Joe Maplin's advice is first class, and of course he's quite right. The world is a better place with a smile.

TED What a great idea for a song. *(He sings operatically)* The world's a better place, with a smile...

GLADYS Oh, shut up, Ted.

TED and SPIKE slip black card into their mouths to black out their teeth.

JEFFREY *(enthusiastically)* Well, tomorrow's Saturday, but we need not wait till then, let's start now. It's quite simple, and what a difference it makes. *(He puts on a false cheesy grin. He turns to GLADYS)*

GLADYS does the same.

GLADYS Well, go on, Yellowcoats.

The Yellowcoats all put on false grins.

BARRY Right, with me, dear. A one, two, a one, two, three, four.

BARRY and YVONNE both put on a grin and end it just as quickly with a look of derision.

GLADYS You too, Ted.

TED and SPIKE both smile with blacked-out teeth.

JEFFREY *(turning to* **MR PARTRIDGE***)* Now come on Mr Partridge, you can do better than that.

MR PARTRIDGE *(unsmiling; rising out of chair)* Nahhhh, sod off!

MR PARTRIDGE walks out of side door. The other staff pat or ruffle him on his way out.

JEFFREY Now, please, we all have our jobs to do, so let's all get on and, er, hi-de-hi!

ALL *(not too enthusiastically)* Ho-de-ho!

JEFFREY goes towards his office.

The others depart except **TED, SPIKE, YVONNE** *and* **BARRY**.

The lights come up on the office.

TED Come on, Spike, where's you bin?

SPIKE Very funny, Ted. Are you going to help me get this off? *(He tries to take the dustbin off)*

TED I "refuse" to do it. D'you get it?

TED leaves.

SPIKE Ted! Ted! Come back Ted!

SPIKE follows **TED** *out.*

BARRY and **YVONNE** *approach* **JEFFREY** *as he enters the office.*

BARRY Mr Fairbrother, might we have a quick word?

JEFFREY Yes, yes, by all means, come in.

They all go into the office.

The lights go down on the staff room.

JEFFREY Pull up a chair.

YVONNE *sits and* BARRY *pulls a spare chair to the table.*
JEFFREY *sits.*

JEFFREY Now, what is it? Do you have an idea for the pool wheeze?

BARRY No. We received this "note" from chalet maintenance. *(He holds out a note)*

YVONNE Most awful grammar.

BARRY It says that we are to stop putting up wallpaper in our chalet.

JEFFREY Well, yes, I believe it causes damage to the walls.

YVONNE We don't paste it up, Mr Fairbrother, how could it possibly cause damage to the walls?

JEFFREY Well, I asked the very same question. Apparently you stick it up with sellotape, and when this is removed at the end of the season it leaves little squares of paint. *(He uses his hands to illustrate the square)*

BARRY We have to do something, the chalets are so depressing. It's like living in Parkhurst.

YVONNE And it's very good quality wallpaper, it's cabbage roses. Pink on a beige background. Your predecessor, Mr Babberstock, never minded, he just used to turn a blind eye to it.

BARRY Mind you with those roses we all had to turn a blind eye.

YVONNE You're only saying that because you wanted gold regency stripes. So common and *nouveau riche.*

BARRY All I was saying—

JEFFREY Yes yes yes, all right. I don't think we should get involved at this stage with what sort of paper it is. What concerns us is the damage.

BARRY How would it be if we put the paper up with drawing pins?

JEFFREY Well surely that would still cause damage?

YVONNE Yes, but only tiny holes.

BARRY We could fill them in afterwards.

JEFFREY Yes, well, I mean that seems a fair enough compromise. I'll get on to maintenance about it.

They all rise.

YVONNE Thank you, Mr Fairbrother, our chalet is so important to us. It's our refuge. Our oasis in the desert of vulgarity.

BARRY *replaces the chair.* **YVONNE** *and* **BARRY** *leave.*

The telephone rings. **JEFFREY** *picks up the receiver.*

JEFFREY *(on the telephone)* Hello, Jeff—

The phone continues to ring—it is the other phone. **JEFFREY** *replaces the receiver and picks up the other one.*

(on the telephone) Hello, Jeffrey Fairbrother speaking. *(Pause)* Yes, yes, I see, well... *(Pause)* You had better put her through. Ah, hello, Mrs West. *(Pause)* Yes. *(Pause)* Yes, but wh—what precisely is the problem you want the camp hypnotist to help you with, Mrs West? *(He rubs his hand over his head with embarrassment)* Well, in, in, in that case, wouldn't it be better if your husband saw him? Yes. Yes, I think so. I'll have a word with him. No. Not with your husband— the camp hypnotist. Yes, thank you. Good—goodbye. *(He replaces the receiver)*

The lights come up on the staff room.

HILARY BOVIS, *a smartly dressed middle-aged woman with a handbag, enters the staff room by the back door with the* **BAILIFF** *who carries a briefcase. She sees* **JEFFREY**'s *door, indicates to the* **BAILIFF** *to remain in the staff room, then knocks at the door.*

BAILIFF *reads notices etc. while* **HILARY** *is in the office.*

JEFFREY *(almost absent-mindedly)* Yes, yes, please come in.

    HILARY *goes into the office.*

HILARY Is this the Entertainment Manager's office?

JEFFREY Er, yes, yes, I'm Jeffrey Fairbrother—can I help you?

HILARY *(closing the door)* I'm Hilary Bovis.

JEFFREY Ted's wife?

HILARY Ex-wife.

JEFFREY *(amazed)* Well, how very nice to meet you. *(He stands)*

    They shake hands.

Please, please, sit down.

    HILARY *sits.*

(sitting) Is he expecting you?

HILARY Is he on the camp?

JEFFREY Why, yes, of course he is.

HILARY Then he's not expecting me.

    JEFFREY *is looking intently at* **HILARY** *as she removes her gloves.*

What are you staring at?

JEFFREY I'm sorry, sorry. It's just that Ted has told me so much about you.

HILARY I bet he has. There's two sides to every story, you know. A comedian's wife runs a close second to his mother-in-law.

JEFFREY Oh, I'm sure your mother's charming.

HILARY No she isn't, she's a cow. He got that bit right.

    TED *enters by the back door, nods towards* **BAILIFF** *and knocks and enters the office.*

TED Jeff, can I talk to you abou— *(Seeing* **HILARY***)* Oh, er, I'll come back later. *(He goes to leave)*

HILARY Come here, Ted!

TED *(slowly coming back in—now very nervous)* Hello, Hilary, you're looking bonny. How are you keeping?

HILARY *(getting up)* Poor.

TED Sorry to hear that. Sciatica bothering you again?

HILARY No, I just haven't got any money.

TED There's a lot of people suffering from that. That Macmillan says we never had it so good. He's totally out of touch.

HILARY I haven't had a penny from you for over three months.

TED What are you talking about? I sent you a money order only last, er, wait a minute. *(To* **JEFFREY***)* Who did I give it to to post?

HILARY Ted, it's me you're talking to. Your time's up.

> **HILARY** *goes to the door and opens it.*

Will you come in, please.

> **BAILIFF** *enters the office, holding the briefcase.*

There he is. *(She indicates* **TED***)*

BAILIFF Are you Edward Bovis?

TED Me friends call me Ted.

BAILIFF Take this, please, sir. *(He hands* **TED** *a large envelope)*

HILARY He's a bailiff, Ted.

JEFFREY Oh, would you like me to leave?

> **TED** *opens envelope to reveal official-looking documents.*

TED It's a bit late for that. I wondered what you were doing out there. I thought you were auditioning for a comic.

The **BAILIFF** *reacts and leaves.*

HILARY *closes the door behind him.*

SPIKE *enters as the* **BAILIFF** *leaves and sits in the armchair.*

HILARY That's a court order, Ted. You've got one week to cough up fifty quid. I'll be down next Friday to collect it. And if you don't divvy up you'll be in the nick.

TED Hilary! Jeff, can you do something?

HILARY *collects her gloves and bag as she departs.*

JEFFREY I'm sorry, Ted, I didn't realize. *(To* **HILARY***)* Let me escort you to the gates, Mrs Bovis.

JEFFREY, HILARY *and the* **BAILIFF** *leave by the back door.*

TED *looks at the paperwork, sighs and steps into the staff room where* **SPIKE** *is sitting.* **TED** *hands* **SPIKE** *the paperwork.*

The lights go down on the office.

TED Would you believe it? That's all I need.

SPIKE *(reading papers)* This is serious you know, Ted. If you don't come up with that fifty pounds by Friday, you'll be inside.

TED She's always sending summonses—not always in person, mind.

SPIKE This one's different. This is the real thing!

TED That's women for you. One minute they promise to love, honour and obey, next minute they're putting you in clink.

SPIKE You must have loved her once.

TED Yes I did. Twenty-sixth of March nineteen fifty-one. *(Pause)* About three o'clock I think it was.

SPIKE What are you going to do about it?

TED What can I do about it? I haven't got fifty quid.

SPIKE Show us your wage packet. I know you've got it, I was there when you collected it.

TED reaches for his pocket and pulls out a wage envelope.

TED There's not fifty quid in there.

SPIKE takes the envelope.

'Ere, what are you doing?

SPIKE opens the envelope and sorts out notes.

SPIKE Right, now. Eleven pound ten. I'll keep eleven pounds, you take ten bob as pocket money.

TED What are you talking about?

SPIKE *(taking money from his own pocket)* And there's nine pound from me that I'm lending you—because I'm an idiot. That makes twenty quid.

TED *(pleased)* Spike, I just don't know what to say.

SPIKE Don't say anything. Just think of the way you are going to come up with the thirty pounds.

TED Well, tomorrow's Saturday, and we get a new batch of naïve campers in. I can try a few of my fiddles. The fixed raffle, the dodgy tombola, the—

SPIKE *(stopping him)* Ted, I don' want to know.

TED Well, there's just one thing that would help me.

SPIKE What's that?

TED Could you give me just another quid for beer money?

SPIKE pushes TED away. They get up and walk towards the back door.

SPIKE Go on!

TED   Don't be like that, just because you are in a position of power.

SPIKE *and* **TED** *exit.*

Blackout.

Tabs.

Scene Two

"Radio Maplin" Desk. Afternoon.

The lights come up on GLADYS *at the radio desk. She plays the notes C G E on the xylophone.*

GLADYS *(expressionless)* Good afternoon, campers, hi-de-hi!

"Ho-de-ho!"

Now don't forget to be in the canteen early for your evening meal, as Fred Larkin, our cordon blue cook, is in an Italian mood. He has conjured up for you, spaghetti bolognese. *(Pause)* And chips. Mmmm, scrumptious. Oh, and one thing more. This evening at eight o'clock sharp it's Egyptian Night, in the Hawaiian ballroom. To the music of Bert Swanley and the Debonaires. See you there. Hi-de-hi!

"Ho-de-ho!"

GLADYS *collects up her papers.*

MR PRITCHARD *enters from the side tabs and stands almost to attention opposite* GLADYS. *He is dressed in a pair of dark trousers, white shirt, black tie and a tank top. He is carrying a bottle wrapped in brown paper.*

GLADYS Oh! What are you doing here? This is private, no one's allowed in here.

PRITCHARD I'm sorry, it's the only way I could get you alone.

GLADYS I beg your pardon?

PRITCHARD There's no cause for alarm, there's something I have to get off my chest. *(He clears his throat nervously)* I have been coming here for three years, just because of you.

GLADYS Oh. That's nice.

PRITCHARD The fact is, to put it in a forward, plain manner. I love you.

GLADYS Oh.

PRITCHARD I dream about you day and night. Seeing me
dressed like this you might not realize that I'm a sergeant
in the Metropolitan Police, C division. So I have to be very
circumspect. Well, I shan't bother you anymore, but I want
you to have this. *(He puts the bottle on the counter top)*
Well. That's all.

> **PRITCHARD** *turns and leaves, closing the door behind
> him.*

GLADYS *(calling after him)* Thank you! *(She reaches for the
bottle and unwraps it)* Oh! Well I never. Champagne.

Blackout.

Open tabs.

Scene Three

Staff Room and Office. Later that afternoon.

The lights come up on **JEFFREY** *and* **PEGGY** *in the office.
There is a dinner jacket, fez and a small "Hitler"-sized
moustache with clips on.* **JEFFREY** *is on the telephone.*
PEGGY *is dusting and generally getting in the way.*

JEFFREY Yes, yes, yes, Mrs Russell, I do appreciate your
dilemma, and I have the chalet maid with me now, and
she's searched it very thoroughly once again but I'm afraid,
afraid your teeth have not come to light. No. *(Pause)* No.
(Pause) No, no. Would you like to speak to her personally?

He covers the mouthpiece and hands the telephone to
PEGGY.

(whispering) Have a word with her, Peggy.

PEGGY *(on the telephone; shouting)* 'Allo! Peggy Ollerenshaw
'ere. *(She pauses while listening)* I've had a real good look,
Mrs Russell, but they're not there, honest. Did you take 'em
out in any other place besides your chalet? Didn't you notice
you hadn't got 'em in when you left? *(Pause)* Oh, I see. *(She
covers the mouthpiece and whispers to* **JEFFREY***)* She's got
two pairs. *(Back to the phone)* Were they National Health
or private? *(Pause)* Oh. Did you have them insured? Oh, I
am sorry. Don't give up hope, there's one last chance. They
empty the swimming pool at the end of the season. Perhaps
they'll turn up in the sump. And if I find them before that,
I'll hand them personally to Mr Fairbrother.

JEFFREY *reacts.*

Yes, right, yes. T'ra. *(She puts the phone down)* Poor woman.
She says the pair she's got is only good for soup.

JEFFREY Well, well thank you for trying, Peggy.

PEGGY Thank goodness I've got you alone, Mr Fairbrother. I've tried to see you again and again, but they won't let me near you. I can do it. *(Pause)* I know I can do it. *(Pause)* Just answer me one question. Is there anything wrong with these legs? *(She lifts her coat up to reveal her legs)*

JEFFREY *(getting up to have a look)* Well, no, no, no, nothing at all. What's all this got to do with me, Peggy?

PEGGY Well, you hold the key to my fate. You could be me first step to stardom. I want to be a yellowcoat.

PEGGY undoes her coat to reveal she is wearing a yellowcoat shirt and shorts.

Gerraload o' this. *(She picks up the telephone receiver from the desk and uses it as a microphone)* Hi-de-hi, campers! Let's hear it for Peggy! Hi-de-hi! "Ho-de-ho!" You're going to have the time of your life this week. The ugly face competition. *(She makes an ugly face)* The knobbly knees competition. *(She wobbles her knees about)* The bonny bouncing baby competition. And the Mr Universe competition. *(She puts down the receiver and adopts a strongman pose)* And at night, in the ballroom... *(She sits on the edge of the desk, facing JEFFREY)*

JEFFREY is astounded, still standing.

...I throw away the clown's mask and become a sophisticated, alluring femmy fatale.

PEGGY gets off the desk and picks up the receiver again. She begins to sing the first verse of "SAND IN MY SHOES" by Bobby Short. She then puts the receiver down on the desk, moves round to the window and sits on the desk, pushing her feet up into the air.

JEFFREY can't bring himself to watch and looks out of the window.

PEGGY *sings the chorus of "SAND IN MY SHOES",*
moving to the far end of the desk halfway through.

The lights come up on the staff room.

GLADYS *enters through the back door and into the office.*
MR PARTRIDGE *wanders in after her into the staff room.*

GLADYS Peggy!! What do you think you are doing here? And
where did you get those clothes from?

PEGGY I borrowed them from the girls.

GLADYS Well put them back at once. And if this happens again
I shall report you to the supervisor.

PEGGY Not Miss Cathcart?

GLADYS Yes, Miss Cathcart.

PEGGY Oo 'eck.

PEGGY *collects her coat and leaves.*

JEFFREY *sees the receiver on the desk. He picks it up,*
detects something on the line and gingerly holds it to
his ear.

JEFFREY *(on the telephone)* No, it's quite all right, it's just, y—No,
no, I don't need any help. Yes, well, she's... *(Pause)* Sorry?
No, I wouldn't say she's that. Th-thank you. *(He replaces*
the receiver on phone)

GLADYS She's a nuisance, that girl.

JEFFREY No, no, weren't you being rather hard on her?

GLADYS Well, if she's that determined to be a yellowcoat she
can go through the proper channels, I won't have her
bothering you. There's too many people round here ready
to take advantage of your soft heart, you need protecting.

JEFFREY Well that's very good of you, Gladys, and I appreciate it.

GLADYS Oh. It's nice to be appreciated.

JEFFREY Yes, well er, is Mr Partridge here?

GLADYS Yes, I think he's outside. Anything important?

JEFFREY Yes, it's very serious, Gladys. The er, camp director had a letter from a couple staying last week saying that Mr Partridge hit their little boy. I've been asked to sack him.

GLADYS Oh dear. Poor Mr Partridge. How's he going to get another job at his age?

JEFFREY Yes, I know, it's most unpleasant. I wish to get it over with as quick as possible. Would you, er, would you send him in.

GLADYS *(worried)* Yes, all right. *(She opens the office door)* Would you come this way, Mr Partridge, please.

MR PARTRIDGE *enters, hands in pockets, with a dejected look.*

GLADYS *pulls out a chair at* **JEFFREY**'s *desk.*

JEFFREY Sit down, Mr Partridge, please.

MR PARTRIDGE *sits and* **JEFFREY** *signals for* **GLADYS** *to go.*

GLADYS *goes, closing door behind her, and exits by the back door.*

Mr Partridge, I don't know how to tell you this.

MR PARTRIDGE You can save your breath. It's about that flippin' kid I hit, isn't it?

JEFFREY Yes.

MR PARTRIDGE Well it wasn't my fault, I was provoked.

JEFFREY Well what happened exactly?

MR PARTRIDGE Well, I was packing up the Punch and Judy and I couldn't find the sausages. So I looked around and there was this snotty-nosed kid, sucking an ice cream cornet.

"Have you got my sausages?" I said. "Get lost Grandad," he said, and I could see the sausages peeking out of his pocket. So I grabbed them off him, snatched his ice cream cornet, stuck it in his face and give it a twist. Then I clipped him round the ear 'ole and kicked him up the arse.

JEFFREY *(ironically)* Yes. *(Looking at letter)* Well, the parents certainly haven't exaggerated the incident, Mr Partridge. Erm, I'm very sorry to have to tell you this, but I've been instructed to dismiss you.

MR PARTRIDGE *(dumbfounded)* Do you mean I've got me cards?

JEFFREY Yes, I'm afraid so.

MR PARTRIDGE Well, that is marvellous that is. That's gratitude for you. After twelve years! Twelve years of trying to amuse those rotten little brats.

JEFFREY Mr Partridge, if you dislike children so, why is it you're a children's entertainer?

MR PARTRIDGE Well, it's a living, isn't it? I was on the halls for years, you know. Whimsical Willie, the Juggling Joker. Then, when after I come out the army in nineteen eighteen, well, things were never quite the same, so I gave up the juggling and became a comic. Then the talking pictures came out, things went from bad to worse. I finished up doing the Punch and Judy, well, it was all right at first, posh parties, kids with their hair in ribands and Eton collars. Then the war came and I went back as a comic doing my act for ENSA. Went to North Africa, France—followed the troops everywhere. And now I finish up with this lot. God, it's pathetic, isn't it?

JEFFREY *(staring at MR PARTRIDGE during his speech)* I think that's fantastic.

BARRY, YVONNE, TED, SPIKE, FRED, SYLVIA, TRACY, BETTY, DAWN *and* GARY *filter in during the ensuing dialogue and assume meeting positions.*

MR PARTRIDGE Eh?

JEFFREY I mean what a marvellous, marvellous career. *(Getting up)* Mr Partridge, I'm going to give you a second chance. If I go to the camp director and take personal responsibility for you, will you give me your word of honour that this sort of thing will never happen again?

MR PARTRIDGE *(standing to shake his hand)* Well of course I will, Mr Fairbrother. You're a trooper, Mr Fairbrother, a trooper.

JEFFREY Thank you very much.

MR PARTRIDGE *(going to leave)* Don't you worry, Mr Fairbrother, I won't let you down.

JEFFREY waves MR PARTRIDGE off with a silly look of satisfaction as he leaves the office.

GLADYS enters.

MR PARTRIDGE joins the others in the staff room.

GLADYS Well, I bet you're glad that's over? I always think it takes a man with great strength of character to give a man the sack. Shall I get on to London for a replacement?

JEFFREY No, that won't be necessary, Gladys, I've given him another chance. *(He stands, rubbing his hands together in a satisfied way)*

GLADYS Ooh! You're all heart. So sensitive. With so much feeling. It's no surprise to me, you can tell by the way you use your hands.

JEFFREY smiles then realizes he has been using his hands and tries to find other things to do with them.

GLADYS leaves the office and joins the staff in the staff room. JEFFREY comes out of the office.

PEGGY *rushes in from the back door, holding another envelope.*

PEGGY Oh, I'm glad you're all here, I thought I might miss yer. I've just come from the admin block, 'ere's another letter for you, Mr Fairbrother. It's from Joe.

GLADYS Mr Maplin to you, Peggy. Give it here.

PEGGY hands over the letter. **GLADYS** *gives her a look and* **PEGGY** *makes her way to the back of the group.*

JEFFREY Gladys. Letter.

GLADYS Oh, sorry. *(She hands* **JEFFREY** *the letter)*

JEFFREY I expect Mr Maplin would like me to read it out straight away, normally I like to read it first. *(Opening the letter)* So erm, please excuse any, erm, hesitations. *(Reading)* "It's getting bigger and bigger. My empire." My empire's getting bigger and bigger. *(Reading)* "That boring Chancellor of the Exchequer says we need to export, so I am exporting Maplin fun, and larking about. I'm starting up a venue for Yank holiday makers on an island at Bahamas." I expect he means, in the Bahama group. In, not at. *(Reading)* "Called San Martin. I've asked the Queen if I can change the name by deed poll to San Maplin. The locals are a lot of bone idle, rum drinking layabouts, who sit around all day doing sweet f—" Er, I, I, er you know. *(He looks up and smiles nervously. Reading)* "So I'm shipping in my best girl yellowcoats from each camp. Whoever wins the Most Popular Girl Yellowcoat Competition will find herself hi-de-hi-ing under a palm tree in two weeks flat."

TRACY Just think, all that sun and sand! Blue seas, white surf and waving palms.

PEGGY emerges from the back.

PEGGY Excuse me, Mr Fairbrother. If one of the girls is going to the Bananas, there'll be a vacancy for a yellowcoat, won't there?

JEFFREY Yes, yes, Peggy, I expect there will be.

PEGGY Can I be considered, please? Well, I don't want to be pushy but I've done ever such a lot of things for you around the camp, and, and I just think I ought to be considered.

TED I think Peggy's right. It's about time she got a chance.

ALL Hear! Hear!

PEGGY *(humbled)* Thanks. I don't know what to say. I'm going to cry—I'll have to go.

PEGGY goes out of the side door.

JEFFREY Gladys, Gladys, tell her of course I'll put her up for it. *(Looking at his watch)* Now, time's getting on, and we have to prepare ourselves for the Egyptian Night, so I'll leave the rest of the points until tomorrow. And so, erm, hi-de-hi!

ALL *(quietly)* Ho-de-ho!

JEFFREY Jolly good.

JEFFREY goes into the office.

All file out of the staff room by the nearest door. The girl yellowcoats jump around excitedly as they leave.

GLADYS goes out of the side door to collect the bottle of champagne.

The lights go down on the staff room.

JEFFREY opens the window of his office and breathes in deeply. He puts on the dinner jacket then tries on the fez (facing the audience as if facing a mirror). He places it on his head and pushes it on. He then lifts the moustache with clips on and tries to clip it on his nose. After some effort it stays. He looks at himself, almost pleased, but he sneezes and it comes off again.

GLADYS *enters through the side door carrying the bottle of champagne and two glasses. She goes into the office.*

GLADYS *(on seeing* **JEFFREY***)* Oh. That's nice. You look like a film star, all romantic and mysterious.

JEFFREY I always feel there's something about a fez that makes one look—degenerate.

GLADYS Oh no, you could never be that. Masterful, perhaps.

JEFFREY *(pointing at the bottle)* What have you got there?

GLADYS It's a present, from an admirer. *(Sitting at the desk)* I do have them, you know. *(She begins to open the bottle)*

JEFFREY I'm sure you do, Gladys. You're not opening it now, are you?

GLADYS Well of course I am. If I share it out amongst all them yellowcoats we'd only get a thimbleful each.

JEFFREY Well, I don't think that we...

GLADYS Well you can't expect me to drink it all by myself, now can you?

GLADYS *cracks the bottle open. [It bubbles over]. She pours out two glasses.*

Oh, we are feeling frisky tonight.

JEFFREY Well, champagne is rather a favourite of mine, Gladys.

GLADYS Come on, it will do you good. After all, *(handing* **JEFFREY** *a glass)* there's only three glasses each.

JEFFREY Well, cheers, Gladys.

GLADYS Cheers.

JEFFREY *stands and looks out of the window.*

JEFFREY I've been thinking. A whole season in the Bahamas could add a whole new dimension to your life.

GLADYS *gets up and goes towards the filing cabinet or duty board. During the next speech,* JEFFREY *turns and listens intently to* GLADYS.

GLADYS Well, I'm not sure I want to go in for that competition this year. There's so many things to keep me here. Family obligations, emotional ties, expectations. No, I won't go in for it this year. It's only fair that I should give some of the other girls a chance—now and then.

The telephone rings. JEFFREY *picks up the receiver absent-mindedly and puts it to his ear. It carries on ringing—it is the other phone ringing. He puts down the receiver and picks up the other one.*

JEFFREY Hello. Hello, Jeffrey Fairbrother. *(Pause)* Oh, Mr Maplin, how unusual to speak to you in person. *(Pause)* Yes, I've just read out your letter to the entertainments staff. *(Pause)* No, no, no I didn't posh it up. I read it as you wrote it, word for word. *(Pause)* Yes. *(Pause)* Yes. *(Pause)* Wh—who, me? *(Pause)* Well, how exciting, well, I'm, I'm overwhelmed, and rather honoured. *(Pause)* Well, thank you very much for telling me, yes. *(Pause)* And goodbye to you too. *(He replaces the receiver)*

GLADYS What was all that about?

JEFFREY That was Joe Maplin in person.

GLADYS I know that. What did he say?

JEFFREY It's about this new camp. He wants an Englishman out there as Entertainments Manager, and erm, I'm on the shortlist.

GLADYS No, you're joking.

JEFFREY Well why should I be joking? In fact it's a very short shortlist. It's between me and a Dick Meadows at Camber Sands.

GLADYS Oh, you'll get it for sure. It'll be a walkover. Dick Meadows is as common as muck. *(She goes to leave)*

JEFFREY Where are you going?

GLADYS *(turning and making for the door)* I want to get to work on those campers. I'm going to win that competition.

JEFFREY But I thought you said you didn't want to go?

GLADYS Well, I've changed my mind, haven't I? It's a woman's privilege. Women don't get many privileges 'round here.

    GLADYS *looks* **JEFFREY** *up and down and leaves.*

    JEFFREY *looks on with a look of suspicion.*

    Blackout.

    Tabs.

Scene Four

A Side Area of The Ballroom. Evening.

The lights come up on a quiet area of the ballroom. **FRED**
and **MR PARTRIDGE** *are at one table, centre.* **SPIKE** *and*
TED *and* **BETTY** *and* **DAWN** *are at two tables around
the bar, right. The bar has a rail around it.* **YVONNE**
is sitting at a table left. The lights are brighter on **TED**
and **SPIKE**'s *table.*

A glitter ball is spinning and distant **"GOODNIGHT
CAMPERS"** *music can be heard.*

SPIKE *is counting out some money on the bar.*

SPIKE Well, however much I count it, Ted, I can't make it more
than forty quid. She'll be here in a couple of days and you're
ten quid short.

TED Well I can't think of anything else—I've done the lot,
chalets, raffles, bingo, and the chewing gum up the paying-
out flute of the fruit machine.

SPIKE *(holding up his hand)* I don't want to hear about it. I'm
only holding on to this money because I don't want to see
you go to jail.

TED I'll tell you what, I've got a dead cert in the two thirty
tomorrow, lend us a fiver and I'll—

SPIKE Oh no, I'm not letting go of this money until I can hand
it over personally to your wife.

TED You're a hard man, Spike.

DAWN We've got your interests at heart, Ted.

BETTY None of us want to see you go to jail.

SPIKE You see. You'll just have to think of something else.

TED I know, give us a quid and I'll buy us a pint while you're working it out.

SPIKE No!

JEFFREY wanders across unsteadily still wearing his fez, with a half pint glass of beer.

TED Are you all right, Jeff?

JEFFREY Yes, perfectly, it's just that there are some lads from my old university who will insist on buying me drinks and I don't know how to refuse.

TED *(looking at* **SPIKE***)* I have to try a bit harder than that to get a drink!

SPIKE He ought to be careful, he's had half a bottle of champagne with Gladys before he came out.

JEFFREY wanders off. Ad lib business.

The lights dim on **TED** *and* **SPIKE***'s table and come up on* **YVONNE***'s table.*

BARRY *comes across from the audience left carrying two elaborately decorated drinks, passing* **JEFFREY***.*

He places the drinks on the table with **YVONNE***.* **YVONNE** *hands him some money.*

BARRY What's this, dear?

YVONNE No, Barry. I'm paying.

BARRY Oh. This is an unexpected surprise. Here's—looking at you.

They raise their glasses and drink.

YVONNE Barry, I've been thinking. I'm going to enter for the most popular girl yellowcoat competition.

BARRY But you're not a yellowcoat, dear.

YVONNE Well I'm wearing one now, and I do many of those boring yellowcoat duties, thanks to you not reading the contract properly in nineteen fifty-six...

BARRY It wasn't my fault. Our agent was supposed to read it. I couldn't read it, I didn't have my glasses with me when we signed it.

YVONNE Oh yes you did. They were in your top pocket. You were too vain to put them on.

BARRY You wouldn't stand an earthly competing with all those young girls.

YVONNE All they have is youth. I have charm, sophistication, experience—and breeding. Americans love that sort of thing, that's why they have English butlers.

BARRY Well, supposing by some fluke of chance you do manage to—scrape—your way home and win, what am I supposed to do while you're lolling about in the Bahamas with those American millionaires and their English butlers?

YVONNE You can always find another partner, until I get back.

BARRY *(loudly)* Oh! That's charming!

YVONNE Keep your voice down, Barry.

BARRY *(quieter)* That's charming. After all I've done for you!

YVONNE Oh, I see. After all you've done for me? May I remind you that when I first took you up, you were a third-rate chorus boy. I taught you everything. I taught you how to dress, how to speak, how to stand up when a lady enters the room. I stopped you using your table knife like a pen. I even allowed you to use my family name, Stuart-Hargreaves...

BARRY And what a mouthful that is. Yvonne and Barry Stuart-Hargreaves...

YVONNE And just how far do you think you would've got in this profession with a name like Bert Pratt...

BARRY That's right. Tell the whole camp.

YVONNE You don't like to be reminded about Bert Pratt, do you?

BARRY Will you keep your voice down!

The lights dim on **YVONNE** *and* **BARRY**'s *table and come up on* **MR PARTRIDGE** *and* **FRED**, *who are looking on.*

MR PARTRIDGE Look at 'em. Look at 'em. Hissing at each other like a couple of vipers.

FRED They ought to ship them out to the Bahamas. You'd have the palms waving, the sea roaring, and them moaning.

MR PARTRIDGE I'd do well out there, you know. I reckon my act would be a novelty for them American kids.

FRED What, Punch and Judy? It's too corny.

MR PARTRIDGE No, no, I adapt my act according to my audience. I'd have Punch as a gangster, Judy as his Moll, and instead of having, er, sausages, I'd have hamburgers. And instead of a policeman, I'd have an American cop. *(In an American accent)* "Ten four, give me the facts man, give me the facts."

FRED I wouldn't go if they asked me. My horses just wouldn't stand the trip.

MR PARTRIDGE They wouldn't take your horses, they'd have new, American horses.

FRED I can't start to get to know new horses at my time of life.

The lights even out.

PEGGY *rushes in from audience left dressed in her "off duty" attire.*

PEGGY Yvonne, Ted, Spike, Barry, Fred! I'm going to be a yellowcoat! Me dream's come true!

FRED That was a bit sudden, wasn't it?

PEGGY Well, Mr Fairbrother did it. He were on to head office to ask about a replacement for the girl who's going to the

Berheimias, and they said it were up to him, so he's given it to me! Oh, he's a lovely man.

FRED Well done, Peggy, you deserve it.

PEGGY Oh, thanks. Well, will yer have a drink?

> **YVONNE** *and* **BARRY** *decline and depart by the side tabs.*

FRED
MR PARTRIDGE } *(together)* Oh yes!

PEGGY Everyone have a drink! Drinks all round—I'm paying! *(She checks her purse)* Oh, 'eck, I've only got half a crown.

TED It's all right, Peggy, we're off now.

> **TED** *and* **SPIKE** *depart.*

> **JEFFREY** *staggers into view holding a glass of tomato juice, very much the worse for wear.*

PEGGY Are you all right, Mr Fairbrother?

> **GLADYS** *enters and approaches* **JEFFREY** *and* **PEGGY.**

(to **GLADYS***)* I don't think he's very well. It could be Fred Larkin's Neapolitan spaghetti bolognese, they're going down like flies.

GLADYS That'll be all, Peggy. I'll deal with this.

> **PEGGY** *departs left. The others except* **GLADYS** *also depart, looking on idly.*

> **JEFFREY** *is now holding on to the rail around the bar as if on a ship.*

GLADYS *(to* **JEFFREY***)* Are you all right?

JEFFREY *(slurring)* ...Perfectly.

GLADYS What have you been drinking?

JEFFREY *(after a pause)* 'Mato juice. These fellows kept buying it for me.

GLADYS *picks up the glass and tastes it.*

There's nothing wrong with 'mato juice.

GLADYS *(pulling a face; realizing it has been spiked)* They've put vodka in here. How many of these have you had?

JEFFREY *(after a pause)* Thousands.

GLADYS You're drunk! I'd better get you out of here before many more see you.

GLADYS *tries to lead* JEFFREY *away, but he won't let go of the rail.*

Let go.

GLADYS *tries to prise* JEFFREY's *hand off the rail. Part of the rail comes away with* JEFFREY *still clinging on to it with both hands.*

They both walk unsteadily off (ad-lib).

The lights fade to blackout. The music fades out.

Open tabs.

Scene Five

Staff Chalets. Later the same evening.

A composite set comprising two chalets. One is JEFFREY's, *the other the Stuart-Hargreaves'. They are lit to indicate lighting outside the chalets. In* JEFFREY's *chalet there is a bed with sheets and a pillow on it, a bedside table with a flannel on it and a window with curtains closed. In the Stuart-Hargreaves' chalet there are two beds, two tumblers, a dressing table with items including an award on it, two towels and a window with curtains closed. The walls are partially covered in garish roses wallpaper.*

The lights come up on the Stuart-Hargreaves' chalet. YVONNE *and* BARRY *are putting up/adjusting their wallpaper. Both are now in their night attire.*

YVONNE A little higher, Barry. Your stalk should be lined up with my flower.

BARRY It's happened before, dear, and it'll happen again.

YVONNE It's so nice of Mr Fairbrother to allow us to pin our wallpaper up. I couldn't stand those dreary walls for a whole season. I hate plain walls. I hate plain anything.

BARRY *(turning, drily)* Me too.

JEFFREY and GLADYS arrive at JEFFREY's chalet.

YVONNE and BARRY hear them and get two tumblers and press them to the wall.

GLADYS opens the door with keys. The chalet is still in semi-darkness, lit by the light outside. JEFFREY still has the rail in his hand and tries to get it through the door.

GLADYS Now be sensible, Jeff.

GLADYS *turns the rail sideways, but* JEFFREY *returns it to horizontal, so it lodges again.*

Let go, Jeff. Jeff, will you let go.

They go into the chalet.

YVONNE He's got Gladys in his chalet.

BARRY Well, she's been trying long enough.

YVONNE But she's asking him to let go. I think we ought to go in and help her. She's changed her mind.

BARRY *(drily)* Remember I changed my mind in digs at Bolton and nobody came to my rescue.

YVONNE Come away, Barry. It's none of our business.

They put their tumblers away and get into bed.

The lights go down on the Stuart-Hargreaves' chalet. They come up slightly in JEFFREY's *chalet.*

GLADYS *puts* JEFFREY *on his bed. She softly closes the chalet door and checks his forehead. She removes his jacket and swings his legs on to the bed. He ends up the wrong end, feet on the pillow. He is still clutching the rail.*

GLADYS Oh, you're so hot.

JEFFREY Gladys.

GLADYS *(standing at the end of the bed looking down on him)* Yes.

JEFFREY Why are you upside down?

GLADYS *(getting a flannel from the bedside)* I do hope nobody saw us coming in. I've got my reputation to think of. *(She places the flannel on his forehead)*

JEFFREY Ah. What lovely cool hands you've got, Gladys. They're all wet.

    GLADYS *collects the pillow and puts it under* **JEFFREY**'s *head.*

GLADYS Up.

JEFFREY Tomatoes.

    GLADYS *sits on the bed beside* **JEFFREY** *and looks him up and down.*

GLADYS Now, what are we going to do with you? Eh?

    Blackout.

    Tabs.

End of Act One

ACT II

Scene One

Staff Chalets. The following morning.

The lights come up on the Stuart-Hargreaves' chalet. The curtains are open. In JEFFREY's *chalet the lighting is very dim and the curtains are closed. He is asleep in the same position, still clutching the rail under the bedclothes, but now minus his shirt and jacket.*

Rousing music is playing from the tannoy.

We hear a knock at a door from offstage.

PEGGY *(offstage)* Mr Partridge, it's laundry morning. Have you got any laundry?

MR PARTRIDGE *(offstage)* Sod off!

PEGGY comes on with a trolley with laundry on it. She knocks and enters the Stuart-Hargreaves' chalet. She collects two towels and replaces them with two clean ones from the trolley.

She notices their items and an award on the dressing table.

PEGGY Oh, they've got such lovely things. *(She picks up the award; to the audience)* And the award for Actress Of The Year goes to... Peggy Ollerenshaw. *(She makes applause noise herself)* Thank you, thank you. *(She holds her hands up)* Ladies and gentlemen, winning this award would not have been possible but for the brilliant writing and direction of my drunken husband. And above all, you, my fans who made a humble little girl from Lancashire into a great international star. *(She bows and makes applause noises again)*

TED *pokes his head around the door. He is wearing trousers and a dirty vest.*

TED It's not worth pinching, it's only tin.

TED *enters the chalet.*

PEGGY Oh, hello, Ted. *(Putting the award down)* What do you want? —And whilst you're here you can take your clean sheets from the trolley *(She indicates the trolley outside)*

TED Have you a spare sink plug as well? Ours has gone missing.

PEGGY What again? That's five this season already. You're not flogging them to the campers are you?

TED *(he has!)* Er, no, no, of course not, I think Spike uses them for his costumes or something.

PEGGY I'll see what I can do. Miss Cathcart won't be happy.

TED Thanks, Peggy.

TED *goes to leave.*

PEGGY I hear you're in trouble, Ted.

TED *(pausing at the door)* Too true.

PEGGY Look, I've had a good week, what with the washing, tips and one thing or another, well, here's a pound. *(She takes a pound from her overall and offers it to* **TED***)*

TED That's very nice of you, but it won't make any difference.

PEGGY Well every little helps. You're very welcome.

TED If I need it I know where to come.

PEGGY Well it's there if you want it.

They both go to leave.

If you do go to jail, I'll come and visit yer.

TED Thanks. you can bring me a pork pie with a file in it.

PEGGY Oh yeah!

> **PEGGY** *shuts the chalet door, collects a laundry bundle and moves to* **JEFFREY**'s *chalet. She knocks and enters carrying laundry. She puts it down and opens the curtains.*
>
> *The lights come up on* **JEFFREY**'s *chalet. They dim down in the Stuart-Hargreaves' chalet.*

PEGGY Hello. Hi-de-hi! (*She notices* **JEFFREY** *is the wrong way up. She looks down at his face*) What are you doing upside down? You look terrible. I bet you won't eat that spaghetti bolognese again. Why have you got this pole in bed with yer? (*She picks up the rail from under the sheet and reacts severely to seeing a "naked"* **JEFFREY** *underneath*) Sorry! Oh! I didn't know you slept in the buff. (*She collects her laundry bundle, dropping a large bra not visible to the audience on the bed, and goes to the door*) I'll do your room later. Good job Gladys was there to see you got back to your chalet safely. (*She slams the door*)

JEFFREY (*sitting up slowly; realizing what was said*) Oh lord.

> **JEFFREY** *sits up and realizes he has nothing on. He looks down at himself under the sheet. He notices the bra lying next to him on his bed. He picks it up with his thumb and forefinger.*

Oh, no!

Blackout. The music stops.

Tabs. (Set change to staff room and office in Act II, Scene Four)

Scene Two

The Ballroom Stage, later that morning.

TED, DAWN, TRACY, BETTY *and* **GARY** *appear in front of the tabs. The girls have voting slips.*

Follow spot on **TED.**

TED *(as the jovial host)* Hi-de-hi, campers!

"Ho-de-ho!"

Ted can't hear you, hi-de-hi!

"Ho-de-ho!"

As you know, we've got the Miss Yellowcoat competition later, so the girls— *(Seeing* **GARY***)* I beg your pardon, Gary. I didn't see you there! The yellowcoats are going to come amongst you with the voting papers. We'll tell you what to do later. *(Looking at no one in particular)* Hello, Mrs Cardew, third year running? Nice to see you back again.

The Yellowcoats go amongst the audience distributing voting slips. **TED** *ad libs—depending on the time it takes.*

Now don't lose your papers, you only get one chance to vote and all votes count! C'mon, Yellowcoats, hurry up. *(Once they are all done)* Thank you very much, ladies and gentlemen, I'll see you later.

Blackout.

Scene Three

"Radio Maplin" Desk. Later that morning.

The lights come up on SYLVIA *at the desk, leaning back in the chair, reading a record cover. There is pop music playing on the record player. She takes the record off the record player. She looks around the desk and finds the xylophone stick. She attempts the* **"HI-DE-HI"** *tune but fails a couple of times, each time mimicking* GLADYS.

GLADYS *enters just after her second attempt.*

GLADYS What are you doing in here?

SYLVIA Jeff suggested I should do some announcements.

GLADYS Mr Fairbrother to you. I'm always making suggestions about you, none of them seem to get adopted. And get your hand out of your pocket.

SYLVIA He thinks I've got just the right tone of voice to wake the campers up.

GLADYS You've no such thing. Your voice is dead common. I have had my instructions from Mr Fairbrother to smarten up you yellowcoats, so I can make things very hard for you.

SYLVIA If you don't, will Jeff make it hard for you?

GLADYS I don't know what you mean. Now, away with you.

SYLVIA *leaves.*

GLADYS *sits at the desk and moves a couple of things back in their place. She plays the notes C G E on the xylophone.*

Good morning, campers, hi-de-hi!

"Ho-de-ho!"

This is Gladys Pugh, your sports organiser. What a packed programme we have for you today. At nine o'clock by the olympic-sized swimming pool we have the blindfold bicycle race, followed by the "Who Can Eat The Most Cake Without Being Sick" competition. We haven't forgotten our younger campers, as we have the "Whose Baby's Got The Biggest Head" competition at ten o'clock in the Mickey Mouse Grotto and the Spaghetti Eating contest in the canteen at eleven. Our older campers should assemble in the Hawaiian Ballroom at ten thirty sharp for the Team Gurning contest. There's a Western theme in the restaurant this lunchtime, as Fred Larkin, our cordon blue chef, has prepared for you baked beans in barbeque sauce. *(Pause)* With sausages. Hi-de-hi!

"Ho-de-ho!"

Tabs.

Scene Four

Staff Room and Office. Lunchtime the same day.

The lights come up on the staff room. SYLVIA, BETTY, TRACY *and* DAWN *are lounging about, reading magazines and filing their nails etc.*

PEGGY *enters from the side door.*

PEGGY I've got your clean laundry out here, girls, d'you want me to put it in your chalets?

BETTY Yes please, Peggy.

PEGGY 'Ere, you know all that fuss Gladys was making over breakfast about me losing her bra. Well it was just a cover up...

TRACY She accused you of pinching it.

PEGGY I know, you know, I mean it's ridiculous. What would I do with one of her bras? *(Looking down)* Anyway, you'll never guess where I found it.

TRACY ⎫
DAWN ⎬ *(together)* No, where?

PEGGY In Mr Fairbrother's chalet.

ALL Oh. No!

SYLVIA Just, lying around?

PEGGY No. Well... *(She gets them to come closer)* ...I was clearing out his chalet, and he left his cufflinks out, so I thought I'd hide them in case they got nicked. Well, I had to go right to the bottom of his drawer to hide'm, didn't I? And underneath this big book, *The Ruins of Petra*, was her bra!

SYLVIA How did it get there? We ask ourselves.

PEGGY Well I reckon he disrobed her in a moment of sudden passion and unbridled lust. And after she left the scene of the seduction, a wave of remorsing guilt swept all over him. Well, men are like that aren't they? And he furtively hid it.

BETTY Oh, so what, good luck to him, I say.

PEGGY No, you don't understand. As soon as he tires with her, he'll be on the prowl for a new victim for his lust. None of us will be safe!

SYLVIA Don't worry, Peggy, if the worst comes to the worst, one of us'll sacrifice ourselves to save your honour.

PEGGY *(chuffed)* Would you? *(Realizing)* Yes, you would, wouldn't you.

PEGGY *departs via the side door.*

TED, SPIKE, FRED, BARRY *and* **YVONNE** *enter quickly.* **SPIKE** *is wearing a funny baby costume under his coat (not visible yet).*

GLADYS *enters last, holding a clipboard.*

GLADYS *(looking at her watch)* Now, I have your jobs for today. *(Looking at her clipboard)* Betty, you take the tiny tots cake eating competition. And erm, you, Sylvia, can take the ugly face competition. I'm sure you'll make a good job of it.

SYLVIA Thank you, Gladys. I expect you'll be doing the knobbly knees contest yourself.

GLADYS *(glaring at* **SYLVIA***)* That'll be all.

JEFFREY *enters from the side door. He is upright, just, and walking very gingerly he makes his way across the staff room.*

JEFFREY *(now centre)* Good morning, everybody.

ALL *(very loudly)* Morning!!

JEFFREY *winces. Just before the office he turns. The staff are eager to respond to the catchphrase.*

JEFFREY Er, hi-de, er, no.

GLADYS *(at the door)* I've been through the programme for today, Mr Fairbrother.

JEFFREY Thank you. *(He turns to the others)* I'm sorry I'm late, everybody. I forgot to wind up my alarm clock.

The lights come up on the office. JEFFREY *goes in.*

TED Forgot to wind up his alarm clock? He were legless.

BARRY From the commotion I heard coming from the chalet last night he may well have been legless, but he certainly wasn't armless. *(He looks at* GLADYS*)*

GLADYS Isn't it about time you all went about your business. *(She claps her hands)*

GLADYS, TED *and* SPIKE *follow* JEFFREY *into the office.*

The others disperse slowly.

The lights dim on the staff room.

JEFFREY *has his head in his hands as they enter, but rises quickly.* GLADYS *grabs two boxes from the filing cabinet and puts them on the desk.*

JEFFREY Ahh! What's this for?

GLADYS This is how we choose the sponsors for the girls in the competition. The girls are here. *(She indicates one box)* And the sponsors here. *(She indicates the other box)*

JEFFREY I'm a bit, er, will you please explain to me how all this works.

TED Well it's the same in every camp. The host, that's me, presents the show in the ballroom, the girl yellowcoats come on one at a time and are introduced by a different member of staff who give some sort of build-up—they're the sponsors. Spike, you pick the girls and Gladys'll pick the sponsor. We have to make sure everything is fair and above board, and we have to be especially careful, what with the winner going to the Bihamas.

SPIKE Any news about you getting that job, Mr Fairbrother?

JEFFREY No, I haven't heard a thing.

GLADYS Oh, you're bound to get it. Spike, pick the first name.

SPIKE *picks a name out of the box.*

SPIKE Betty.

GLADYS *picks a name out of the box.*

GLADYS Her sponsor is Fred Quilly.

SPIKE *(picking a name out)* Tracy.

GLADYS *(picking a name out)* Her sponsor is Mr Partridge.

SPIKE *(picking a name out)* Sylvia.

GLADYS *(picking a name out)* She's drawn you, Spike. You'll have a job making her sound attractive.

SPIKE *(picking a name out)* Yvonne.

GLADYS *(picking a name out)* Barry.

JEFFREY Well, she can hardly complain about that.

SPIKE *(picking a name out)* Gladys.

GLADYS *(picking a name out)* You'll have to do me, Jeff.

JEFFREY Well, let's hope you win it again, Gladys.

GLADYS Don't worry, I'm taking no chances. There's three days until the final. We'll see who's the most popular yellowcoat on the camp. Those girls won't see my heels for dust.

TED Right, we must be off, we're doing the baby with the biggest head competition—show him, Spike.

SPIKE *drops coat to reveal comic baby costume and completes it with a hood and large dummy.* **TED** *produces a large pincer gauge.*

JEFFREY *(putting his head in his hands)* Oh, my God.

SPIKE *and* **TED** *both leave by the back door.*

GLADYS Oh. By the look of you, you could do with a black coffee. Shall I get you one?

JEFFREY No, no. I'll sort myself out. I er, I feel I ought to apologize to you about last night.

GLADYS *(sitting on the opposite side of desk)* Oh no. You've got nothing to apologize for.

JEFFREY Haven't I?

GLADYS Those campers laced your drink. It wasn't your fault you were—a bit tiddly.

JEFFREY Tiddly? I was drunk, Gladys.

GLADYS Nonsense. You knew what you were doing. *(Pause)* Most of the time.

JEFFREY *gets up and nervously moves around the office, then faces the audience.*

JEFFREY Gladys. I can remember you helping me back to my chalet. But after that it's all a bit—hazy. What time did we get back to the chalet?

GLADYS I dunno. Not long after "Goodnight campers", about twelve o'clock.

JEFFREY So you left me at about...at about, what...at about ten past twelve?

GLADYS *(tidying the desk)* Oh I dunno, I think it was a bit later than that.

JEFFREY Well, how much later, Gladys?

GLADYS I don't know. You don't look at your watch, do you?

JEFFREY Did, did anyone else come in?

GLADYS No.

JEFFREY *(walking round* GLADYS *to the far end of the desk)* Gladys, look. I don't normally get into that state. But on the rare occasions that it has happened before, I always take two Alka Seltzers, and erm, get into my pyjamas. *(He mimes getting into pyjamas)*

GLADYS You didn't do any of that.

JEFFREY Yes, I, I, I know Gladys, when I woke up this morning I wasn't wearing my...

GLADYS Weren't you now?

The lights come up on the staff room.

BETTY *enters the staff room, goes to the office, knocks quickly and opens the door.* JEFFREY *almost falls over as if trying to "put on pyjamas".*

BETTY Sorry to interrupt. They're waiting for you to referee the bicycle hockey, Gladys.

GLADYS Oh, heavens, yes. I'll be there directly.

BETTY *exits.*

JEFFREY *is by the window looking out, still in a state of shock.*

JEFFREY Well, look, I'm terribly sorry about this, Gladys, and it won't happen again.

GLADYS What do you keep apologizing for? You were all right. Some people, when they've had a few drinks, turn nasty. You were just the opposite.

JEFFREY *(turning round)* You, you mean I, I was...

GLADYS You were lovely. You just got rid of some of your... inhibitions.

JEFFREY *turns back again.*

It made a nice change to see you...without your stiff...upper...lip.

GLADYS *gets up to go as* **JEFFREY** *turns around. Not knowing what to do or say,* **JEFFREY** *puts his head in his hands.*

GLADYS *leaves by the back door.*

FRED *enters the staff room by the side door and goes to the coffee table. He sniffs his clothes, then looks under his shoes. He is just about to wipe them on a tea towel.*

JEFFREY *emerges from the office.*

JEFFREY Hello, Fred. Can you do me a black coffee, please.

FRED Good idea. *(He pours out the coffee and hands it to* **JEFFREY***)* You can't beat it when you've had a skinful. Old Partridge swears by it.

JEFFREY *smiles.*

I've been meaning to ask you, Mr Fairbrother, Can I change my day off next week to Tuesday?

JEFFREY I'm sure that'll be all right, Fred.

FRED *sits in the armchair.* **JEFFREY** *sits in another chair.*

FRED This pal of mine, Reg, ex jockey, is getting married again. He works at the Isle of Wight camp. To tell you the truth, he's had to get married. He's put one of the yellowcoats in the club.

JEFFREY Club?

FRED Yes, you know, the family way. Joe Maplin made him do the right thing. He's a tartar for morals, is Joe. One whiff of scandal and he has them marching up the aisle. He once had security as best man. Mind you, if you ask me, she's planned it. She's been after him for two seasons. And now she's got him. Reg doesn't know the half of it. He hasn't met his future mother-in-law yet. I have. You know it's amazing how these pretty girls have these dragons for mothers. Last season, Gladys had her mother down here for the day. You wouldn't believe it. Nice woman, mind, I'm not saying anything against her, but you know how Gladys has got a nice... *(He illustrates her figure)*. I mean she's properly stacked. Her mother's out here. *(He stretches out his arms)* With a moustache. Fancy a biscuit with that? *(He gets up)*

JEFFREY   Er, no, no thank you, Fred. Tell me, I'm concerned about Ted. Do you know if he's managed to raise enough money to pay his alimony?

FRED   He's doing ever so well, Mr Fairbrother, he's got nearly forty pounds.

JEFFREY   Forty pounds!? How did he manage that?

FRED   He's pulled in a lot of favours and things. Spike's been keeping an eye on him. Er, well, I must be going, Mr Fairbrother, I've got to feed my horses, they need their oats at this time of day, they don't get much out of life and you know what they're like if they don't get their oats.

JEFFREY   *(to himself)* In a strange way, I don't even know if I've had mine.

FRED   *(turning)* Sorry?

JEFFREY   Oh, nothing. Thank you, Fred.

Blackout.

Tabs.

Scene Five

The Ballroom Stage. Three days later.

Contest in front of tabs and audience. PEGGY *is on stage with a ballot box.* GARY *and* DAWN *place two microphones in front of tabs and stand left.*

TED *comes on through the curtains.*

Follow spot on TED.

TED *(to the audience)* Hi-de-hi!

"*Ho-de-ho!*"

Ted can't hear you. Hi-de-hi!

"*Ho-de-ho!*"

And now the moment you've all been waiting for. The Most Popular Girl Yellowcoat of the Season Contest.

The girls GLADYS, YVONNE, SYLVIA, BETTY, TRACY *come on from left, and their sponsors* JEFFREY, BARRY, SPIKE, FRED *and* MR PARTRIDGE *come on from right with notes. They line up behind* TED.

Now, you've all got your voting papers. When you've seen all the girls put a tear along the girl of your choice. *(To the audience)* No sir, not on the girl, on the voting paper. Peggy will collect them in a secret ballot box.

PEGGY *moves centre to display the box and walks into audience showing the box. She finishes at the top of seating and stays there.*

First contestant, sponsored by our resident children's entertainer, Uncle Willy, the delightful pocket Venus, Tracy Bentwood.

TED *steps away and* MR PARTRIDGE *and* TRACY *come to the other microphone.*

MR PARTRIDGE *(reading notes)* Now, er, "Tracy Bentwood is twenty-four, she was born in Stoke Newington. Her vital statistics are thirty-six, twenty-three, thirty-six. Her hobbies are tennis, swimming and stewing."

TRACY *(aside)* Sewing.

MR PARTRIDGE Eh?

TRACY Sewing.

MR PARTRIDGE Oh, sewing. *(Aside)* Sorry! *(To the audience)* I think you ought to vote for her because she's a lovely girl who goes around like a ray of sunshine.

TRACY *and* MR PARTRIDGE *go to a position to line up.*

TED Let's give a big hand to Tracy Bentwood! Next, sponsored by our resident jockey, Fred Quilly, the curvaceous Betty Whistler. *(He steps away from the microphone)*

FRED *and* BETTY *come to the microphone.*

FRED *(reading)* "Betty Whistler is twenty-five, born in 'Arrow on the 'Ill. Her vital statistics are forty, twenty-four, thirty-six. Her hobbies are reading Charles Dickens and Jujitsu." *(He lowers the paper)* I think she ought to win because she's a good sport and she don't use the Jujitsu, except as a last resort.

FRED *and* BETTY *go to a position to line up.*

TED Let's hear it for Betty Whistler! Next, introduced by our camp comic, Spike Dixon, the girl you all like to whistle at, but you can't because your tongue's hanging out—Sylvia Garnsey, known to us all as "Legs".

TED *steps away.* SPIKE *and* SYLVIA *come to the microphone.*

SPIKE *(reading)* "Sylvia Garnsey is twenty-five."

GLADYS *(aside to* **JEFFREY**) And the rest.

SPIKE "She was born in Littlehampton, her vital statistics are, thirty-four, twenty-three, thirty-four. She's very sporty, her hobbies are riding, swimming, running, sailing and climbing."

GLADYS *(aside to* **JEFFREY**) He's missed out the main one.

SPIKE *(lowering the paper)* I think you ought to vote for her because she's always laughing, and fooling around to make sure everyone has a good time.

TED Give her a big hand!

SPIKE *and* **SYLVIA** *join others.*

Next, sponsored by her partner, Barry, please welcome Yvonne Stuart-Hargreaves.

TED *steps away.* **BARRY** *and* **YVONNE** *join hands and come to the microphone.*

BARRY Yvonne was born in nineteen fourteen...

YVONNE *reacts.*

...and comes from Southport and her vital statistics are, thirty-four, *(pause)* thirty-four, thirty-four. *[Adjust size to suit actress]* Her hobbies are advising people, character analysis and witty conversation. I think you ought to vote for her because she's "different" from all the others.

TED Let's hear it for Yvonne!

YVONNE *and* **BARRY** *join the others.*

And last, but not least, sponsored by your entertainments manager, Jeffrey Fairbrother, your popular sports organizer, Gladys Pugh.

TED *steps away as* JEFFREY *and* GLADYS *come to microphone.*

JEFFREY *(reading)* "Gladys Pugh is twenty-six."

Yellowcoat girls stifle an audible laugh/splutter.

(reading) "She was born in Pontypridd. Her measurements are thirty-six, twenty-six, thirty-six..." Of course, I haven't checked them.

No laugh.

(reading) "Her hobbies are looking after children, collecting stray dogs and reading to old people." *(He lowers the paper)* I think she should win because she is a genuine, warm-hearted, good person. *(He looks at the paper)* And we all love her.

GLADYS *turns to* JEFFREY *with cow eyes.*

TED Thank you, Gladys Pugh!

GLADYS *and* JEFFREY *join the others.*

Just tear your voting paper next to the girl of your choice and place it in the secret ballot box.

PEGGY *makes her way down through the audience, holding the box, collecting votes.* GARY *and* DAWN *help.*

PEGGY Put yer votes in the box, come on now, hi-de-hi! That's it. *(Ad lib etc.)*

PEGGY *eventually makes her way through side tabs right. As she commences, the girls and sponsors discreetly move out of sight into the wings.*

Blackout.

JEFFREY *and* TED *move behind the bar in the blackout.*

Scene Six

The Bar, left. Later the same afternoon.

The small lamps come up on JEFFREY *and* TED *at the bar, with five piles of paper and a page of notes in front of them.*

JEFFREY *(looking at the notes)* That's twenty-eight for Tracy, thirty-six for Betty... *(Pause)* ...nine for Yvonne and sixty-three each for Gladys and Sylvia. That's one hundred and ninety-eight and one spoiled paper.

TED Well, you'll have to do something. They can't both go to the Bihamas.

JEFFREY This silly person has torn somewhere between Gladys and Sylvia. They must be a complete idiot. *(He shows* TED*)*

TED You do get all sorts in here. But you'll have to make your mind up which name is nearest the tear.

JEFFREY It could be either, Ted. Look. *(He hands over the paper)*

TED You've got a problem there. I'm going back before they get impatient.

TED *gets up to go.*

JEFFREY *(imploring)* Ted, Ted. *(Pause)* I don't know what to do.

TED Jeff. For once in your life, make a decision.

TED *exits.*

Blackout.

Scene Seven

The Ballroom Stage. Later the same afternoon.

The girls and sponsors come on to the same positions as before (no PEGGY*).*

TED *comes through the curtains holding a yellow winner's sash.*

Follow spot on TED.

TED Hi-de-hi!

"Ho-de-ho!"

Sorry to keep you waiting, campers, but for the last hour Mr Fairbrother and I have been incarcerated in the Smuggler's Bar, and that's a nasty thing to happen to anybody. Well, we've finished counting all the votes and here to announce the winner is your popular Entertainments Manager, Jeffrey Fairbrother.

JEFFREY *tries to find a gap in the curtain (ad lib). Just as he does this* GLADYS *attracts* TED*'s attention on stage.*

GLADYS Who's won?

TED I don't know, Jeff had to give the casting vote.

JEFFREY *is helped through the curtain by* TED. JEFFREY *trips as he emerges and stands awkwardly at the mic. He blows into it before speaking.*

JEFFREY Well, ladies and gentlemen, hi-de-hi!

"Ho-de-ho!"

Thank you. It's been a very close run thing, we had to recount the votes several times, and the winner of the Nineteen Fifty-nine Most Popular Girl Yellowcoat contest is... *(Pause)* ...Sylvia Garnsey.

SYLVIA *shrieks with delight.*

SYLVIA I've won! I've won!

SYLVIA *joins* **TED** *on stage. He puts the sash around her and gives her a kiss.* **SYLVIA** *waves at the audience.* **GLADYS** *turns away from the audience in shock.* **JEFFREY** *joins* **GLADYS** *and smiles.*

GLADYS *turns around and slaps* **JEFFREY**, *then storms off.*

JEFFREY Gladys! Gladys! Come back!

Blackout.

The girls and their sponsors exit.

Open tabs.

Scene Eight

Office and Staff Room. Later the same afternoon.

The lights come up on both the office and the staff room. There is a bottle of drink and glasses on the table in the staff room and a cheque on the desk in the office.

GLADYS *storms through the back door and staff room into the office.* **JEFFREY** *is close behind.*

During the next dialogue the others all enter the staff room.

JEFFREY Gladys! What is the meaning of this? What have I done?

GLADYS So! You've got me out of your hair. You're taking Sylvia to the Bahamas with you.

JEFFREY I'm not going.

GLADYS I don't understand you sometimes.

JEFFREY I'm not going, Gladys. There was a telegram this morning. Joe Maplin must have heard the rumours about you and me. I just hope my wife's solicitors don't find out, they'd have a field day.

GLADYS Jeffrey. You gave her the vote so we could stay together.

JEFFREY I had to, I couldn't run the place without you. You're a damn good right hand man.

JEFFREY *taps* **GLADYS'** *shoulder.* **GLADYS** *is still overwhelmed.*

GLADYS Come on, let's join the others, I've arranged an announcement.

They both go into the staff room.

(clapping her hands for attention) Ever since last Monday night, when Mr Fairbrother was the unfortunate victim of circumstance and had to be helped into his chalet, certain vicious rumours have been going around the camp.

All look towards **BARRY**. *He reacts by looking up at the ceiling etc.*

And I mean to put paid to them once and for all. Dawn, there should be a gentleman outside waiting, could you ask him to come in please.

DAWN Yes, Gladys.

DAWN *goes out through the back door.*

YVONNE If you kept your mouth shut, Barry, these sort of things wouldn't happen.

BARRY Yes, but wouldn't it be boring.

DAWN *brings in* **PRITCHARD**. *He is attired in the same manner as before.*

GLADYS This gentleman has something to say to you.

PRITCHARD *turns to* **GLADYS**. *She indicates that he should speak. He stands to attention.*

PRITCHARD Oh. My name is Pritchard. I am a sergeant in the London Metropolitan Police, C Division. *(To* **GLADYS***)* Do you want me to take the oath?

GLADYS That won't be necessary.

PRITCHARD I am here on a week's holiday... *(He gets out a pocket notebook)*

BARRY That's unusual.

PRITCHARD *(reading from the notebook)* On the night in question, at approximately twelve o'clock, midnight, I was proceeding along the chalet lines to my normal quarters when I was apprehended by this *(turning to* **GLADYS***)* young lady, to come to the assistance of *(to* **JEFFREY***)* this gentleman, who I now know as Mr Jeffrey Fairbrother who was in a state of intoxication...

TED *(nudging and miming to* **SPIKE***)* He was pissed.

PRITCHARD Together we placed the gentleman on the bed. Observing that he was of the male gender, I asked her to withdraw and wait outside the door while I undressed him and put him to bed. I then rejoined her and bid her goodnight, and we proceeded to our separate chalets. This was approximately twelve minutes past twelve... *(Turning the page)* a.m. *(He closes the notebook)*

GLADYS Thank you, Sergeant Pritchard. *(To the group)* Any questions?

They all look at each other.

PRITCHARD I shall now proceed in enjoying my holiday. If any of you would care to join me in a game of clock golf, I would only be too willing to give you a good thrashing.

PRITCHARD *turns and leaves.*

The others watch him leave.

GLADYS That'll be all. Now you can continue with your celebrations.

JEFFREY *(uplifted)* Yes, yes, that'll be all.

JEFFREY *and* **GLADYS** *enter the office, closing the door behind them. The staff get drinks etc. and share them out in the staff room.*

The lights go down on the staff room.

Well, I'm glad that's over, Gladys. What a good job that policeman was passing.

GLADYS Yes. He was convincing, wasn't he?

JEFFREY Yes, he was very con— *(Realizing)* What do you mean, Gladys?

GLADYS Perhaps he only said it to help me out.

JEFFREY Gladys! Do you mean to say you got that policeman to perjure himself?

GLADYS He didn't perjure himself. He was on holiday.

JEFFREY *(in shock)* Gladys. I have to know. I mean, did you...?

GLADYS Jeffrey Fairbrother! Do you think I would take advantage of you when you were drunk? I'm not a cad you know. I wouldn't make you do anything you didn't want to do.

JEFFREY I'm all confused again. *(He sits at the desk)*

GLADYS Oh dear. You're all confused again. And you, a university professor. I'm only a simple girl from the valleys. And I'm not confused. I know exactly what happened.

The lights come up on the staff room.

GLADYS *haughtily turns and leaves, going through to the staff room.*

JEFFREY *gets up and follows her through to the staff room. The others cheer and give them both a drink.*

JEFFREY Ah. Well, here's to you, Sylvia.

ALL Cheers!

TED You'll have to pack all your things, you know. Just think, ten more days and you'll be soaking up all that sun.

GLADYS I'm glad you've won. I really am.

TED I expect you'll be getting some fancy gear in London to take with you.

SYLVIA Well, no. I'm going to go via New York. The clothes there are great.

MR PARTRIDGE You wanna watch yourself in New York. It's full of muggers and hoods. A bit like Luton. *[Or local reference]*

BARRY Ted, I never did ask. How many votes did Yvonne get?

TED It were very close.

YVONNE How close?

TED Let's put it this way. If your fan club hadn't got himself locked in the toilet, you might have got double figures.

> **PEGGY** *emerges from the back, coming in through the side door. She is holding a large paper bag.*

PEGGY Mr Fairbrother, as Sylvia's going Wednesday week, can I take over the ballroom on Tuesday night?

JEFFREY Well, yes of course you can, Peggy.

SPIKE Is that your coat?

PEGGY Yes. It's just been finished. I had it especially made.

FRED Put it on!

PEGGY Shall I?

ALL Yes, go on. *(Etc)*

PEGGY Oh...

> **PEGGY** *takes the yellow coat out of the bag and puts it on over her dust coat.* **SPIKE** *helps her. When it's on, all the others cheer with light applause.*

Oh, it's lovely stuff. I can't believe it. It's like a dream.

> **PEGGY** *moves to back of stage to show her coat to a couple of the girls.*

TED Well, let's put some music on! Spike, turn on the radio.

> **SPIKE** *turns on the transistor. The others talk excitedly amongst themselves. It is the end of the news.*

ANNOUNCER ...for the future weather. Bad storms are affecting the Bahamas where hurricane Angela is causing mass destruction on the smaller islands.

JEFFREY Sshh, hang on a minute, Spike, turn it up.

SPIKE *turns up the volume.*

During the announcement PEGGY *leaves by the side door leaving her coat behind on the back of a chair.*

ANNOUNCER One of the most seriously affected has been San Martin, especially its north tip. This is the location of the new Maplin Holiday Camp, which took over two years to construct. It was completely destroyed within two hours. From his home in Hampstead, Mr Maplin said, "Fate's clobbered me and that's a fact. I never had none of this at Camber Sands." Cricket. And at Lords today, England struggled yet again...

JEFFREY Turn it off, Spike.

SPIKE *turns off the radio. All the staff are looking down.*

BETTY *(putting her arm around her)* Oh, Sylvia...

JEFFREY Oh, how awful. I am sorry.

SYLVIA I don't believe it.

FRED Never mind. He'll rebuild it. Joe won't be beaten.

SPIKE It'll take another two years!

SYLVIA I might not win next time.

TED Then there's Peggy. What about poor Peggy?

They all look around. PEGGY *is nowhere to be seen.*

JEFFREY Where's she gone?

SPIKE Well, she was here a minute ago.

GLADYS Look!

They part and we see **PEGGY**'s *yellow coat draped over the chair near where she was standing.*

JEFFREY Oh dear.

SPIKE Mr Fairbrother, I think we should all go and look for her—she'll be in a terrible state.

JEFFREY Yes, yes. I quite agree, Spike. Girls, you take the chalets, and boys, you search the Mickey Mouse Grotto and the canteen. She can't have gone far.

ALL Yes, Mr Fairbrother.

All except **TED** *leave by the nearest door.*

TED *is just about to leave when* **SPIKE** *and* **HILARY** *enter by the back door.*

SPIKE Your wife's here, Ted.

TED Oh, 'eck. I forgot it were today.

HILARY *enters.*

Hello, Hilary.

HILARY Right, Ted, where is it?

SPIKE *(reaching into his pocket)* I've got it here, Mrs Bovis. It's ten pounds short, I'm afraid, but he has tried ever so hard.

SPIKE *hands over the money, hesitates, then exits by the back door.*

HILARY What's going to happen to the other ten pounds, Ted?

TED That's all there is, you've got the lot. I haven't even had a drink this week.

HILARY All right, I'll settle for this. To tell you the truth, it's more that I expected. I'll tell them you've paid in full, you'll not go to jail this time.

TED Thanks, Hil. I'm glad you've still got a soft spot for me.

HILARY I haven't. I'm just being practical. *(Looking around)* So this is it, eh? Going to be a big star. Rolls Royces. Penthouse flats in Park Lane. Now look at you. Same old shabby jacket. You're pathetic.

TED Have you done?

HILARY It's your ego, Ted. You just wanted to get up on stage and be admired, a lot of people cheering you on instead of getting a decent job and doing a decent day's work like everybody else. It's like when you were mouthing off about that big part in television—whatever happened to that?

TED What, with Granada Television? It were for a weekly drama called *Coronation Street*—I've heard nowt since and not likely to either—it were a non-starter. They were just wasting my time.

There's a knock and **JEFFREY** *enters by the back door.*

JEFFREY May I come in?

TED Yeah. She's just leaving.

JEFFREY As a matter of fact, it's your wife I want to see. Er, look, Mrs Bovis, I understand that Ted is ten pounds short. Here is a cheque on my personal account to make up the difference. *(He hands a cheque over)* I'll sort it out with Ted later.

HILARY You're a jammy devil, Ted. You're a con man and a liar, and a twister, but you'll always manage to find someone who's a soft touch to help you out. I'll be back.

HILARY *turns and leaves by the back door.*

JEFFREY *is all smiles. He thinks he has done his duty.*

TED *(annoyed)* What did you have to go and do that for? I mean I'm speechless.

JEFFREY *(affronted)* How about saying thank you?

TED Thank you? I've just done a deal with her. She's just accepted forty quid, now I owe you a tenner!

JEFFREY *(equally annoyed)* Well, yes! And God knows when I'm going to get it back!

TED You're going to get it back right now. *(He pulls a wad of notes from rear pocket and removes two £5 notes)*

JEFFREY *(shocked)* Where did you get that from?

TED I had a book going on the Miss Yellowcoat competition, and thanks to you, I'm quids in!

JEFFREY *is lost for words and storms out.*

Jeff! Jeff! There's no need to be like that! Jeff!!

TED *follows* JEFFREY *out, calling his name.*

After a second or two, PEGGY's *head appears out of the side door and looks around furtively.*

She enters the staff room, picks up her yellow coat and goes to centre stage. She is sniveling.

The lights fade. Follow spot on PEGGY.

PEGGY I'm going to do it—I can do it. One day I'll become a yellowcoat. *(Putting on the coat)* I'm going to try and try, I won't give up. I've got what it takes. *(Brightening up)* One day, I'll be standing in the spotlight on stage in front of an audience. I'll give'em songs, I'll give'em jokes and I'll send'em away happy, because that's what they've come here for! *(Shouting loudly)* Hi-de-hi, everyone! —Hi-de-hi!

Blackout.

Tabs.

Walk down.

FURNITURE AND PROPERTY LIST

Further dressing may be added at the director's discretion

PROLOGUE

On stage: Radio Maplin Desk Area:
Radio desk. *On it:* xylophone, xylophone stick
Record player. *On it:* record

ACT I
Scene One

On stage: Staff Room And Office
In staff room:
Desk. *On it:* two telephones
Filing cabinet
Duty board
Letter

In office:
Table. *On it:* tea and coffee cups, sugar cubes, tray
Chairs
Armchair
Transistor Radio
Window

Off stage: Pair of trousers (**Peggy**)
Shoulder bag (**Fred**)
Yellow envelope with letter inside (**Gladys**)
Sugar lumps (**Peggy**)
Handbag (**Hilary**)
Briefcase containing envelope with official-looking
   documents inside (**Bailiff**)

Personal: **Ted:** envelope containing notes (in pocket)
Barry: note from chalet maintenance (in pocket)

Scene Two

On stage:	Radio Maplin Desk Area
Set:	Papers (on desk)
Off stage:	Bottle of champagne wrapped in brown paper (**Pritchard**)

Scene Three

On stage:	Staff Room and Office
Set:	In Office: Dinner jacket Fez Hitler-sized moustache with clips
Off stage:	Yellow envelope with letter inside (**Peggy**) Bottle of champagne, two glasses (**Gladys**)
On stage:	Ballroom Side Area: Glitter ball Two tables Bar with rail around it. *On it:* money Chairs Money (for **Yvonne**)
Off stage:	A half pint glass of beer (**Jeffrey**) Two drinks (**Barry**) Glass of tomato juice (**Jeffrey**)
Personal:	**Peggy**: purse

Scene Four

On stage:	Staff Chalets: In Jeffrey's Chalet: Bed. *On it*: sheets, pillow Bedside table. *On it:* flannel Window with curtains closed In the Stuart-Hargreaves' Chalet: Two beds

Two tumblers
Two towels
Dressing table. *On it:* items including award
Garish roses wallpaper
Window with curtains closed

Off stage: Keys (**Gladys**)
Rail from bar (**Jeffrey**)

ACT II

Scene One

On stage: Staff Chalets

Set: In the Stuart-Hargreaves' Chalet:
Open curtains

Off stage: Trolley with laundry, including two clean towels
and a large bra, on it (**Peggy**)

Personal: **Peggy**: pound (in overall pocket)

Scene Two

On stage: Ballroom Stage:
Voting slips

Scene Three

On stage: Radio Maplin Desk Area

Set: Record cover

Scene Four

On stage: Staff Room and Office

Set: In Staff Room:
Magazines
Nail files
Tea towel

In Office:
Two boxes containing pieces of paper (on top of
    filing cabinet)

Off stage: Clipboard (**Gladys**)

Personal: **Gladys**: watch

Scene Five

On stage: Ballroom Stage:
Ballot box

Off stage: Two microphones (**April** and **Dawn**)
Notes (**Jeffrey**, **Barry**, **Spike**, **Fred** and
    Mr Partridge)

Scene Six

On stage: Ballroom Side Area

Set: Five piles of paper (on bar)

Scene Seven

On stage: Ballroom Stage

Off stage: Yellow winner's sash (**Ted**)

Scene Eight

On stage: Staff Room and Office

Set: In Staff Room:
Bottle of drink and glasses (on table)

In Office:
Cheque (on desk)

Off stage: Large paper bag containing yellow coat (**Peggy**)

Personal: **Pritchard**: notebook (in pocket)
Spike: money (in pocket)
Ted: wad of money including two £5 notes (in rear
    pocket)

LIGHTING PLOT

Property fittings required: glitter ball

PROLOGUE

To open: Bring lights up on "Radio Maplin" desk area

Cue 1   **Gladys** and **Yellowcoats** exit
          Fade lights down on the desk area

ACT I, Scene One

To open: Bring lights up on the staff room and office set

Cue 2   **JEFFREY** sits at the desk looking at
          paperwork   (Page 5)
          Fade lights down on the office

Cue 3   **Gladys** knocks on the office door   (Page 8)
          Bring lights up on the office

Cue 4   **Jeffrey** leaves the office   (Page 9)
          Fade lights down on the office

Cue 5   All depart except **Ted**, **Spike**, **Yvonne**
          and **Barry**   (Page 13)
          Bring lights up on the office

Cue 6   All go into the office   (Page 13)
          Fade lights down on the staff room

Cue 7   **Jeffrey** replaces the telephone receiver   (Page 15)
          Bring lights up on the staff room

Cue 8   **Ted** hands **Spike** the paperwork   (Page 18)
          Fade lights down on the office

Cue 9   **Spike** and **Ted** exit   (Page 20)
          Blackout

ACT I, Scene Two

To open: Bring lights up on the "Radio Maplin" desk area

Cue 10   **Gladys**: "Well I never. Champagne."   (Page 22)
          Blackout

ACT I, Scene Three

To open: Bring lights up on the office

Cue 11   **Peggy** finishes the chorus of "Sand In
            My Shoes"   (Page 25)
          Bright lights up on the staff room

Cue 12   **Gladys** goes out of the side door   (Page 30)
          Fade lights down on the staff room

Cue 13   **Gladys** leaves. **Jeffrey** looks on   (Page 33)
          Blackout

ACT I, Scene Four

To open: Bring lights up on the ballroom (side area). The
            lights are brighter on **Ted** and **Spike's** table, right
          A glitter ball is spinning

Cue 14   **Jeffrey** wanders off   (Page 34)
          Dim lights on **Ted** *and* **Spike's** *table*
          Brighten lights on **Yvonne's** *table, left*

Cue 15   **Barry**: "Will you keep your voice down!"   (Page 37)
          Dim lights on **Yvonne's** *table*
          Brighten lights on **Mr Partridge** *and*
            Fred's *table, centre*

Cue 16   **Fred**. "...new horses at my time of life."   (Page 37)
          Even out lights

Cue 17   **Gladys** and **Jeffrey** walk off unsteadily (Page 39)
          Fade lights down to blackout

ACT I, Scene Five

To open: There is lighting outside the chalets

Bring lights up on the **Stuart-
Hargreaves**'chalet

Cue 18   **Yvonne** and **Barry** get into bed   (Page 41)
Fade lights down on the **Stuart-
Hargreaves**'*chalet*
Bring lights slightly up on **Jeffrey's**
chalet

Cue 19   **Gladys**: "...to do with you? Eh?"   (Page 42)
Blackout

ACT II, Scene One

To open: Bring lights up on the **Stuart-Hargreaves**' chalet

Cue 20   **Peggy** opens the curtains in
Jeffrey's chalet   (Page 45)
Bring lights up on **Jeffrey's** *chalet*
Dim lights on the Stuart-Hargreaves'
chalet

Cue 21   **Jeffrey**: "Oh, no!"   (Page 45)
Blackout

ACT II, Scene Two

To open: Bring up spot on **Ted**

Cue 22   **Ted**: "I'll see you later."   (Page 46)
Blackout

ACT II, Scene Three

To open: Bring lights up on the "Radio Maplin" desk area

No cues

ACT II, Scene Four

To open: Bring lights up on the staff room

Cue 23   **Jeffrey**: "I forgot to wind up my alarm
clock."   (Page 51)

Bring lights up on the office

Cue 24   All except **Gladys**, **Ted**, **Spike** and **Jeffrey**
        disperse slowly   (Page 51)
        Dim lights on the staff room

Cue 25   **Gladys**: "Weren't you now?"   (Page 54)
        Bring up lights on the staff room

Cue 26   **Jeffrey**: "Thank you, Fred."   (Page 56)
        Blackout

Scene Five

To open: Bring up spot on **Ted**

Cue 27   The girls and their sponsors move out of
        sight   (Page 60)
        Blackout

Scene Six

To open: Bring small lamps up on the bar

Cue 28   **Ted** exits   (Page 61)
        Blackout

Scene Seven

To open: Bring up spot on **Ted**

Cue 29   **Jeffrey**: "Gladys! Gladys! Come back!"   (Page 63)
        Blackout

Scene Eight

To open: Bring up lights on the office and staff room set

Cue 30   The staff get drinks and share them out   (Page 66)
        Fade down lights on the staff room

Cue 31   **Gladys**: "I know exactly what happened." (Page 67)
        Bring up lights on the staff room

Cue 32   **Peggy** goes to centre stage   (Page 72)

Fade lights. Follow spot on PEGGY

Cue 33   **Peggy**: "Hi-de-hi, everyone!—Hi-de-hi!"   (Page 72)
           Blackout

EFFECTS PLOT

PROLOGUE

Cue 1   To open   (Page 1)
Muffled late 50s music is playing

Cue 2   Gladys lifts the record off the record player   (Page 1)
Music stops

ACT I

Cue 3   **Yvonne** and **Barry** leave   (Page 15)
The telephone rings

Cue 4   **Gladys**: "...a chance—now and then."   (Page 32)
The telephone rings

Cue 5   To open Scene Four   (Page 34)
Distant "Goodnight Campers" music is
     playing

Cue 6   The Lights fade to blackout   (Page 39)
Music fades out

ACT II

Cue 7   To open Scene One   (Page 43)
Rousing music is playing

Cue 8   Blackout   (Page 45)
Music stops

Cue 9   To open Scene Three   (Page 47)
Pop music is playing

Cue 10   **Sylvia** lifts the record off the record player (Page 47)
Music stops

Cue 11   **Spike** turns on the transistor radio   (Page 68)
Voice on tape as per p. 69

Cue 12   **Spike** turns up the volume on the radio   (Page 69)
Voice on tape gets louder

VISIT THE SAMUEL FRENCH BOOKSHOP AT THE ROYAL COURT THEATRE

Browse plays and theatre books, get expert advice and enjoy a coffee

Samuel French Bookshop
Royal Court Theatre
Sloane Square
London
SW1W 8AS
020 7565 5024

Shop from thousands of titles on our website

 samuelfrench.co.uk

 samuelfrenchltd

 samuel french uk